Write your hopes for this study in the form of a prayer.

Father, here is what I hope for from **you**…

_____

_____

_____

_____

_____

_____

Here is what I hope for from the **group**…

_____

_____

_____

_____

_____

_____

Here is what I hope for from the **journal**…

_____

_____

_____

_____

_____

_____

Here is what I hope for from **myself**…

_____

_____

_____

_____

_____

_____

DVD Presentation

Use the space below to write your reflections or thoughts on this episode.

_____

_____

_____

_____

_____

_____

_____

_____

_____

_____

_____

_____

In regard to the concept of AHA, which of the following is closest to your initial feeling?

☐   I know some people who need an AHA in their lives.

☐   I'm glad I've had my AHA in the past, so I'm done with that.

☐   I am probably due for an AHA, but I'm not sure I really want one.

☐   I am probably due for an AHA and look forward to the new life
and freedom it will bring.

DAILY EXERCISES
DAY 1

Only be careful, and watch yourselves closely
so that you do not forget the things your eyes have seen
or let them fade from your heart as long as you live.
— **Deuteronomy 4:9**

Those who don't remember history are doomed to repeat it.
— **George Santayana**

CONTENTS

A MESSAGE FROM KYLE

It's time to wake up.

My guess is that you don't like that phrase very much. Maybe even just reading it makes you cringe. Even if you're a morning person, be honest—hearing your alarm in the morning is most likely not your favorite sound in the world. But what we all know is that, no matter how loud or annoying that sound is in the morning, it's necessary. You can ignore it for a little while, and you can hit the snooze button a few times, but eventually, it's really just time to wake up. In Luke chapter 15, Jesus tells a story about a guy who needed a wake up call. He may not have really been "asleep," but he definitely needed to wake up. It definitely wasn't the sound he wanted to hear, but it was the sound he needed to hear. And when he realizes that there's no more ignoring it and no more snooze button, he finally wakes up to see that God has been waiting for him the whole time. **AHA**.

Whether you've been asleep for a long time and need a louder alarm or if you know it's time to wake up but need a nudge out of bed, my prayer is that this video series produced by City on a Hill will wake you up to see that God has been waiting for you.

I hope that this series will be part of your AHA story.

INTRODUCTION

This study is based on a famous story told by Jesus that has come to be known as "the parable of the prodigal son."

In the parable, the younger of two sons asked for his inheritance even though the custom was for him to receive his inheritance only after his father was dead. Despite the unbecoming nature of the request, his father gave him his share, which was a third of the father's property. The son promptly turned the assets into cash, journeyed to a distant land, squandered the money in reckless living, and ended up broke.

And that is when his **AHA** began.

AHA is an acronym for Awakening, Honesty, and Action, three essential elements for lasting life change.

This journal is designed to serve as a personal companion in your exploration of this powerful parable. But even more importantly, the journal is intended to help you discern if you are in need of a present-tense AHA—and if you are, to guide you in an effective response.

So the first question is this: should you be in need of an AHA—an Awakening that calls for Honesty and Action that leads to lasting life change—are you open to it?

Indicate where your answer falls on this spectrum:

|—————————————————————————————|

Not really   Yes, definitely

What thoughts go through your head that lead you to that answer? Jot them below.

_____

_____

_____

_____

_____

_____

_____

If your answer falls on the "yes" side of the spectrum, this journal offers daily exercises and experiments structured to support you in detecting whether you need a contemporary AHA. And should you need an AHA, helpful guidance is provided for your "journey home."

If your answer falls on the "no" end of the spectrum, then…well, why not do the journal anyway?

Jesus told another parable about two sons. In this story the father told both sons to go work in the vineyard. The first son refused to go but later actually went. The other son agreed to go but never did. Jesus asked his listeners, "Which son did what the father wanted?" The answer, of course, is the first son, even though he balked initially (Matthew 21:28–31).

Though you may be saying no right now, the Father doesn't give up on you. He waits. Your no may yet turn into a yes. So, wherever you are on the yes-no spectrum, give the daily practices in this journal an enthusiastic chance, and discover whatever you find as you go.

You should know that this journal is not a Bible study workbook. For the most part, you won't be asked to look up verses and fill in blanks with answers. Rather, the focus will be on experimenting with daily spiritual practices that help you to:

- see where you are
- decide what to do about where you are
- act on what you decide

The reason for this approach is twofold.

First, we can hide behind Bible study. We look up verses and write down correct answers, all the while staying squarely in a hypothetical, theoretical, abstract world, safely clear of our personal, actual, concrete lives. Most of us are acquainted with Christians who know the Bible backward and forward, but know themselves hardly at all. We can be theologically aware without being self-aware.

Second, AHAs get short-circuited by only knowing information. An AHA must go beyond information to become transformation. If an AHA stays in the academic, theoretical realm, it ends stillborn. A true AHA involves searching self-reflection followed by concrete action. In both 1 Corinthians 11:28 and 2 Corinthians 13:5, believers are urged to "examine" themselves and then to act on what they find.

This journal, then, lines up with the three ingredients of AHA. The daily exercises focus on:

– expanding your awareness so that if you need an Awakening, you can realize it

– increasing your Honesty so that you face reality as it is, not as you might want it to be

– guiding you in appropriate Action that suits the particular journey home from whatever far country in which you may find yourself

Are you ready to step in and discover what you find?

Note your reactions to this introduction on this page and the next.

_____

_____

_____

_____

_____

SESSION

1

MORNING: This week you will be guided to act upon the advice in the Scripture above by recalling AHAs from your past, to see what you can glean.

Today's task is to make a list of the big AHAs in your life so far.

Don't rush. Stroll slowly through the scrapbook of your mind. As you approach this reflection, you might think chronologically, beginning with childhood, then your adolescent years, then your twenties, and so on. Or you could think in terms of locations: homes in which you have lived, churches you've attended, places you've worked, destinations you have visited, or retreats you have taken, for instance. Jot below the AHAs that come to mind.

_____
_____
_____
_____
_____
_____
_____
_____
_____
_____
_____

Write a prayer to your Father expressing what you find yourself feeling and thinking in light of recalling these past AHAs.

_____
_____
_____
_____
_____
_____
_____
_____
_____
_____
_____

As you go through your day, be open to other AHAs coming to mind. If any do, write them down.

_____

_____

_____

_____

_____

_____

_____

_____

_____

_____

_____

_____

_____

_____

EVENING: Did any other AHAs come into view? If so, list them with the others above.

Look over your list and ask yourself these questions:

- Which AHAs were the most dramatic? You might star these.

- Which made the most lasting impact? You might check mark these.

- Which have you forgotten, and the effect is now hardly evident in your life? You might put a question mark beside these.

How do you find yourself led to pray now?

_____

_____

_____

_____

_____

_____

_____

_____

DAY 2

MORNING: Look over the AHAs you listed yesterday. Choose one to reflect on more deeply.

Give this AHA story a title:

_____

Now take a few minutes to replay the story of that AHA in your mind. Make the mental images as vivid as you can. Attempt to re-experience the scenes, the emotions, the various events. Try to go beyond simple recall by re-inhabiting those times, to truly go back in your imagination and actually be there, feel what you felt, think what you thought, see what you saw. Don't rush and shortchange this exercise. Take your time. Absorb all you can from this AHA experience.

****

As you go through your day, hold this AHA in your mind. As you enter various situations, ask yourself, what does my past AHA say about this moment, this event, this interaction?

EVENING: How did keeping this AHA in mind affect your thoughts and actions during the day?

_____
_____
_____
_____

Respond to the following questions about the AHA you relived this morning.

What was your Awakening? Describe it.

_____
_____
_____
_____
_____
_____
_____

What was your Honesty? What truth did you have to tell yourself?

_____

_____

_____

_____

_____

What were your Actions in light of the Awakening and Honesty?

_____

_____

_____

_____

_____

What is the effect of that AHA in your life today?

_____

_____

_____

_____

_____

How are you led to pray after this reflection?

_____

_____

_____

_____

_____

Between now and your next group session, you are encouraged to go to a location where you experienced one of your significant AHAs. This special place might be a hospital chapel, an Alcoholics Anonymous meeting room, a retreat center, or the shoulder of a lonely road. The purpose will be to soak up the atmosphere of that setting and see what memories, thoughts, and feelings are triggered. So be thinking about where you might go, and when.

DAY 3

MORNING: In Acts 26:1–23, the apostle Paul recounted his greatest AHA. Read the passage and then describe Paul's Awakening, Honesty, and Action.

Paul's Awakening was…

_____

_____

_____

_____

_____

Paul was Honest about…

_____

_____

_____

_____

_____

Paul's subsequent Actions were…

_____

_____

_____

_____

_____

Though it may not be as dramatic as Paul's, choose another of your own AHAs to revisit today.

Give this AHA story a title:

_____

As with yesterday, you're challenged to resist the urge to recall the episode in a passing, hurried way. Rather, take several minutes to re-experience the events of your AHA as dramatically as you can.

As you recall your AHA this time, consider finding a memento from that time to hold in your hand. Or flip through a diary from that era. Or play a song connected to the period. Or you may choose this day to return to a destination associated with this AHA and do your remembering and responding to today's questions there.

****

As you go through your day, hold this AHA in the forefront of your mind. As you enter various situations, ask yourself, what does this past AHA say about this moment, this event, this interaction?

EVENING: How did keeping this AHA in mind affect your thoughts and actions during the day?

_____
_____
_____
_____
_____
_____

What was your realization or Awakening in this AHA? Describe it.

_____
_____
_____
_____
_____
_____

How did God speak to you, or what influences or events brought the Awakening about?

_____
_____
_____
_____
_____
_____

How did you react to the initial Awakening? Did you resist it, ignore it, welcome it? Attempt to describe why you reacted as you did.

_____
_____
_____
_____
_____
_____
_____
_____
_____
_____

What was your Honesty? What truth did you have to tell yourself?

_____
_____
_____
_____
_____
_____
_____
_____
_____
_____

What were your Actions in light of the Awakening and Honesty?

_____
_____
_____
_____
_____
_____
_____
_____
_____

How has your life changed as a result of this AHA?

_____

_____

_____

_____

_____

_____

_____

Even though he already knows it, retell the story of this AHA to your heavenly Father in prayer.

DAY 4

MORNING: In 2 Corinthians 12:7–10 we find a very different AHA experience for Paul. What elements of AHA does Paul face in this passage?

_____

_____

_____

_____

_____

_____

_____

_____

_____

_____

_____

_____

_____

_____

_____

_____

Today choose one more AHA to revisit.

Give this AHA story a title:

_____

As with the previous two days, you're encouraged to take the time to fully re-engage the memory, to enter the recollection as completely as you can. You may choose this day to return to an AHA-related destination and do your remembering and respond to today's questions there.

****

As you go through your day, hold this AHA in the forefront of your mind. As you enter various situations, ask yourself, what does this past AHA say about this moment, this event, this interaction?

EVENING: How did keeping this AHA in mind affect your thoughts and actions during the day?

_____
_____
_____
_____
_____
_____

What was your realization or Awakening in this AHA? Describe it.

_____
_____
_____
_____
_____
_____

How did God speak to you, or what influences or events brought the Awakening about?

_____
_____
_____
_____
_____
_____

How did you react to the initial Awakening? Did you resist it, ignore it, welcome it? Attempt to describe why you reacted as you did.

_____

_____

_____

_____

_____

_____

_____

_____

What was your Honesty? What truth did you have to tell yourself?

_____

_____

_____

_____

_____

What were your Actions in light of the Awakening and Honesty?

_____

_____

_____

_____

_____

_____

How has your life changed as a result of this AHA?

_____

_____

_____

_____

_____

_____

_____

_____

Imagine your heavenly Father telling you the story of this AHA from his perspective. Write the story out below as you envision hearing it from him.

_____

_____

_____

_____

_____

_____

_____

_____

_____

_____

_____

_____

_____

_____

_____

_____

_____

_____

_____

_____

_____

_____

_____

_____

_____

_____

_____

_____

_____

_____

_____

_____

_____

DAY 5

MORNING: What Awakening/Honesty/Action patterns do you find in John 8:2–11?

_____
_____
_____
_____
_____
_____
_____
_____
_____
_____
_____
_____
_____
_____
_____
_____

Unlike some stories in John's Gospel, we are not told what Action this woman took after encountering Jesus. Did she change for good? Did she change for a while then go back to her old ways? Did she not change at all? What do you make of this open ending?

_____
_____
_____
_____

Answer some general questions about your past AHAs:

What was the most beneficial aspect of remembering—and reliving—your past AHAs?

_____
_____
_____
_____
_____

Do you tend to hold onto the power and effect of past AHAs or are you more likely to have to experience the same AHAs over and over before really getting them?

_____

_____

_____

_____

_____

Do you have an AHA that is open-ended; that is, how you will ultimately respond is still up in the air? If so, describe it.

_____

_____

_____

_____

_____

_____

Consider whether sharing one of your AHAs might be helpful to you or to the group. You might ask the Holy Spirit for direction.

If you chose an AHA to describe to the group that is different from those you worked on so far, follow the directions from Day 4 for this AHA as well. Write your responses below.

_____

_____

_____

_____

_____

_____

Write a prayer regarding your next group gathering, however you are led to pray.

_____

_____

_____

_____

_____

_____

SESSION

2

MISSING

ANJELA ARZA

THE DISTANT COUNTRY

DVD Presentation

Use the space below to write your reflections or thoughts on this episode.

_____

_____

_____

_____

_____

_____

_____

_____

_____

_____

_____

_____

_____

_____

_____

_____

_____

_____

DAILY EXERCISES

Whoever has ears to hear, let them hear.
— Jesus, Mark 4:9

DAY 1

MORNING: Think through the areas of your life listed below. What, if any, alarms are sounding in each area?

- Family:

_____
_____
_____

- Health:

_____
_____
_____

- Finances:

_____
_____
_____

- Work:

_____
_____
_____

- Spiritual life:

_____
_____
_____

- Other:

_____
_____
_____

If you skipped that last exercise, ask yourself where your resistance comes from. Choose from the possibilities below or write your own.

- ☐ It seems like too much work to think though all that.
- ☐ I fear I will find so many alarms that I will be overwhelmed.
- ☐ I hate introspection. I prefer action.
- ☐ I feel pressure to get on with my day and get things done.
- ☐ I don't want to feel the emotional pain that alarms can trigger.
- ☐ I already know what the alarms are, and I don't think I can fix what they are signaling.
- ☐ Other: _____

How might your wiser self respond to the resistance? For instance, if you are worried that you will be overwhelmed by the sheer number of alarms going off, your wiser self might remind you that acknowledging several alarms is not a commitment to solve the issues all at once, that this exercise is just asking you to notice the alarms, not fix everything today.

_____
_____
_____
_____
_____
_____
_____
_____
_____
_____
_____

As you engage your day, be alert for any other alarms you hear sounding.

How are you led to pray as you enter this day?

EVENING: Did you detect any other alarms during your day? If so, add them to the list from this morning.

Look over each alarm. As you do, notice whether you have a sense of approach or avoidance, a feeling of attraction or aversion, a wanting to explore this alarm or a wanting to ignore this alarm. Put each alarm in one of the columns below.

I feel inclined to
approach and explore
this alarm

I feel inclined to
avoid and ignore
this alarm

_____   _____
_____   _____
_____   _____
_____   _____
_____   _____
_____   _____
_____   _____
_____   _____
_____   _____
_____   _____
_____   _____
_____   _____

How are you led to pray?

_____
_____
_____
_____
_____
_____
_____
_____

DAY 2

MORNING: Where do you see yourself on this spectrum? I tend to…

|—————————————————————————————|

blame myself when things go wrong   blame others when things go wrong
experience a high degree of guilt   experience a low degree of guilt
be hard on myself   be easy on myself

When it comes to perceiving alarms, a person who marked the left side of the spectrum may…

- hear far too many alarms

- take personally alarms actually meant for others

- heed the false alarms of an overactive conscience

For this person, a flat tire becomes a warning not to skip morning devotions again. The flu becomes a sign of unconfessed sin. A job loss indicates God wants to teach a lesson about perseverance. Almost everything is an alarm.

A person on the right end of this spectrum will tend to…

- hear few alarms

- fail to notice legitimate alarms

- think the alarms they do hear are meant for someone else

For the person on the right side of the spectrum, an unhappy wife simply means she is spoiled and needs to grow up. An arrest for drunken driving means the cops are out to get you. A job loss indicates the boss is an idiot. Nearly nothing is an alarm.

If you marked the left side of the spectrum, look back over your alarms you listed yesterday. Do you get the sense you might be overly scrupulous? Are there any false alarms or alarms that can be traced to a hypersensitive conscience? Write your thoughts.

_____

_____

_____

_____

_____

_____

_____

_____

If you marked the right side, think back to when you were considering your alarms yesterday. Did possible alarms come to mind that you quickly dismissed? Are other people pointing out alarms that you aren't taking seriously? If so, list them.

_____

_____

_____

_____

_____

Today, ask a trusted friend about where he or she would put you on the "blame myself / blame others" spectrum. You might also ask this friend about specific alarms you are hearing, whether he or she thinks the alarms are legitimate concerns or whether you are being overly sensitive.

EVENING: Write what your friend said today.

_____

_____

_____

_____

_____

_____

Put the names of several family members and friends on the "blame self / blame others" spectrum found on page 31, according to what you think is accurate.

As you look over the spectrum with its various names, what stands out to you?

_____

_____

_____

_____

The purpose of today's exercises is to help you decide whether the alarms you hear are real and valid or the false alarms of an overactive conscience. Here is an activity that may help:

- **First**, think about what your conscience is like and the things it says to you.
- **Next**, imagine that God is saying exactly what your conscience is saying.
- **Last**, consider what kind of a god that would be. Would he be a wise, good, and loving god, or would it be something else, like a petty, legalistic, picky god, or an apathetic, amoral, disinterested god?

Example A: Let's say a person has a conscience that accuses him anytime he doesn't pick up a piece of stray trash on the street, stop to talk to a lonely co-worker, or stay awake while praying. If God were just as this conscience is, what kind of god would he be? What kind of character would he have?

Example B: Let's say a person has a conscience that rarely speaks up about anything, that never cares when she lies, gossips, cheats on her taxes, or overbills a client. If God were like her conscience, what kind of a god would he be?

1. My conscience says things like…

_____

_____

_____

_____

2. I imagine God being just like that...

_____
_____
_____
_____
_____
_____

3. That kind of God would be...

____ gentle   ____ picky   ____ obsessive

____ indifferent   ____ joyful   ____ tyrannical

____ righteous   ____ legalistic   ____ amoral

____ cruel   ____ understanding   ____ small-minded

Other words you might use/or this god:

_____
_____
_____
_____
_____

After pondering today's questions, which alarms seem to be legitimately important and which do not?

Important Alarms	Unimportant Alarms
_____	_____
_____	_____
_____	_____
_____	_____
_____	_____

DAY 3

MORNING: Look over the various alarms you listed. Does one stand out as particularly loud, important, or pressing? Write it here. If an alarm doesn't stand out, choose one to explore more deeply.

_____

What is this alarm about? What is it trying to tell you?

_____
_____
_____
_____
_____
_____
_____
_____
_____
_____
_____
_____
_____
_____
_____
_____
_____
_____
_____

Was this alarm in the ☐ approach-and-explore column or in the ☐ avoid-and-ignore column from Day 1's exercise?

How long has this alarm been sounding?

_____
_____
_____
_____
_____

Name the various shapes this alarm has taken. For example, in the video, Anjela was accosted by a club patron. Then she was threatened by her boss. Later she vomited on the audience. Each incident was a different alarm. But each alarm was sounding the same warning. These alarms were all related. When it comes to the alarm you have chosen to investigate, do you see other related alarms sounding the same basic warning? If so, write them below.

_____
_____
_____
_____
_____
_____
_____
_____
_____

Have you tried to act on this alarm before? If so, what happened?

_____
_____
_____
_____
_____
_____

What do you find yourself saying to your Father in heaven after responding to these questions?

_____
_____
_____
_____
_____
_____
_____
_____
_____
_____

Today, notice any alarm bells going off associated with your chosen alarm.

EVENING: What are your thoughts and feelings about taking the journey of AHA in regard to this alarm—to become fully Aware, to be Honest, and to Act?

_____

_____

_____

_____

Mark any feelings or thoughts that correspond to yours.

☐ **Hopeless:** I have tried to act on this alarm before and I always fall back.

☐ **Hopeful:** I want to make changes and am excited about a strategy to do so.

☐ **Resistant:** I like where I am despite the issues; I don't want to change.

☐ **Avoidant:** I know I need to change, but I don't want to face the pain that making changes will require.

☐ **Cautious:** I am willing to try, but I know me, that I waffle and am weak.

Try telling your thoughts and feelings to God. As you do, notice which of the four zones from the matrix you view him as occupying.

_____

_____

_____

_____

_____

_____

_____

	COMPASSION	CONDEMNATION
HONEST		
DISHONEST		

DAY 4
MORNING

• What is the far country associated with this alarm? For example, if your alarm is saying, "You're neglecting your family," then the far country might be your job, the bar, the golf course, the TV remote, or all of the above.

_____

_____

_____

_____

• When you go to the far country, what are you running to? What is the allure of this far country? What do you love about it?

_____

_____

_____

_____

_____

_____

_____

_____

_____

_____

• When you go to the far country, what are you running from? For example, Tim was running from the fear of never being somebody big and important, of being a disappointment to his wife. Claire was running from the drudgery of a daily responsibility. Anjela was running from the pressure of financial debt and the idea of being a burden to her dad. What are you running from?

_____

_____

_____

_____

_____

_____

_____

_____

_____

- Running to the far country can be a "hot reaction," that is, impulsive and emotional, like Claire running to Brad. Or running can be a "cold decision," that is, planned and calculated, like Tim scheming to defraud the company. How would you describe your running to this far country? Does it tend to be hot or cold? Explain your thinking.

_____

_____

_____

_____

_____

If you are tempted to go to the far country today, simply notice the attraction, what you are running to; and notice the avoidance, what you are running from.

_____

_____

_____

_____

_____

EVENING: Come to terms with the cost associated with this far country. What is the price in each area listed below?

- Spiritual cost:

_____

_____

_____

_____

_____

- Relational cost:

_____

_____

_____

_____

_____

_____

- Physical cost:

_____
_____
_____
_____
_____

- Financial cost:

_____
_____
_____
_____
_____

- Psychological/emotional cost:

_____
_____
_____
_____
_____

What is it like for you to list these costs?

_____
_____
_____
_____
_____
_____
_____
_____
_____
_____
_____
_____
_____
_____

As you responded to these questions, in which of the four zones did you find yourself when it comes to your disposition toward yourself? Draw a stick figure representing yourself in that zone.

	COMPASSION	CONDEMNATION
HONEST		
DISHONEST		

How do you find yourself led to pray?

_____

_____

_____

_____

_____

DAY 5

MORNING: Today's task is to make a decision about whether you will embark on the AHA journey in relation to the alarm you have been exploring this week. To do so, imagine yourself making the decision while being in each of the four zones.

For example, if you were in the place of being honest with yourself and giving yourself compassion and grace, would you move forward in dealing with this alarm, or would you not?

Next, imagine yourself in the honesty with condemnation zone. If you were honest with yourself while judging yourself and despising yourself, would you move forward or not?

Do this with each zone. Write your inclination inside that area.

	COMPASSION	CONDEMNATION
HONEST		
DISHONEST		

Ask the Father which zone he would prefer you to be in.

If you don't sense a response, based on your knowledge of Jesus his Son, in what zone do you think the Father wants as you consider this alarm? Note your reasoning.

_____

_____

_____

_____

_____

As you go through your day, notice in which zone you find yourself in regard to your own life.

EVENING: Do the same exercise from this morning, but this time imagine **God** being in each zone.

For instance, if you viewed God as compassionate toward you as well as completely honest, would you move forward with facing this alarm?

Or if God were honest with you while shaking his head at you and condemning you, would you move forward?

Write your inclination in each zone of the matrix on the following page.

	COMPASSION	CONDEMNATION
HONEST		
DISHONEST		

Which space do you think God really comes from, and why?

_____
_____
_____
_____
_____
_____
_____
_____
_____
_____
_____
_____
_____
_____
_____
_____
_____
_____
_____
_____
_____
_____
_____
_____

What do you find yourself deciding in regard to moving forward on the AHA journey in regard to your alarm?

_____

_____

_____

_____

_____

_____

_____

_____

_____

_____

_____

_____

_____

_____

_____

_____

_____

_____

_____

_____

_____

_____

_____

_____

_____

_____

_____

_____

_____

_____

_____

SESSION

3

A SUDDEN AWAKENING

DVD Presentation

Use the space below to write your reflections or thoughts on this episode.

_____
_____
_____
_____
_____
_____
_____
_____
_____
_____
_____
_____
_____
_____
_____
_____
_____
_____
_____
_____
_____

	COMPASSION	CONDEMNATION
HONEST		
DISHONEST		

DAILY EXERCISES

DAY 1

MORNING: When it comes to the alarm you have chosen to explore, what is likely to come down the road if you ignore it? There are probably many possible scenarios. This morning's task is to describe the **best possible scenario.**

For example: Claire might marry Brad. They live happily together. She and her daughter, Amber, reconcile. Claire's ex-husband, Walter, remarries someone who actually appreciates him. And God forgives all.

In Matthew 5:45, Jesus said that our Father in heaven "causes his sun to rise on the evil and the good, and sends rain on the righteous and the unrighteous." That is, God gives good gifts even to the undeserving.

If you ignore your alarm, what is the best possible scenario?

_____
_____
_____
_____
_____
_____
_____
_____
_____
_____

After writing this scenario, what do you find yourself praying about?

_____
_____
_____
_____
_____
_____
_____
_____

EVENING: Consider the **worst possible future** should you ignore this alarm.

For example, even if Claire marries Brad, she would likely remain demanding and critical, since past action is the best predictor of future behavior. Brad might escape by drinking more and more until it becomes a daily habit. He might start hitting Claire. She might grow so frustrated that she divorces Brad as she did Walter. Her relationship with her daughter might never recover. Claire could end up alone, full of regret and bitterness. Her heart toward God could get harder and colder so that she remains far from grace.

You might object to considering the worst possible scenario, reasoning that the worst never comes about. But remember the consequences that King David experienced after he slept with the married Bathsheba.

In this darkened state he went on to commit murder. Then the son he conceived with Bathsheba died shortly after birth. Later, when his son Amnon raped his half-sister Tamar, David found himself without the moral courage to confront this dreadful sexual misconduct.

David's inaction led to another son, Absalom, taking matters into his own hands by murdering Amnon. Over time Absalom lost all respect for David and initiated a coup. In the ensuing civil war, Absalom was killed.

The consequences of David ignoring the alarms in his life snowballed to scope hardly imaginable, especially for "a man after God's own heart."

What might be the worst possible scenario should you ignore this alarm?

_____
_____
_____
_____
_____
_____
_____

As you look back at the scenario you just painted, do you detect any denial in the form of minimization? If so, edit your scenario.

After writing this scenario, how do you find yourself being led to pray?

_____

_____

_____

_____

_____

_____

DAY 2
MORNING: Yesterday you described the best and worst scenarios that could come from ignoring this alarm. Today, describe what you consider to be the **most likely scenario.**

For example, Claire would likely marry Brad. It is also likely that over time the shine of this new relationship will wear off and things will become more routine. Brad will likely begin to take Claire for granted. Claire would likely remain entitled and self-centered. Claire has always been dissatisfied and will likely return to being dissatisfied, especially as Brad's attention wanes. Her marriage will end up pretty much where her marriage to Walter ended. Walter will likely work through his anger, hurt, and sadness, and remarry a woman who will appreciate him more than Claire did. But there will always be scars on his heart. Amber, Claire's daughter, will likely soften toward her mother over time, but since Amber appears to be a person of strong convictions, she will probably never really trust or confide in her mom again. Their relationship will be polite but not intimate. Claire will be unlikely to reach out to God, having run so far from him.

Honestly describe what you consider to be the most likely scenario should you ignore your alarm. Include:

- how your character will be affected
- how your relationships will be affected
- how others will be affected

_____
_____
_____
_____
_____
_____
_____
_____
_____
_____
_____
_____
_____
_____
_____
_____
_____
_____
_____
_____

Look back over the scenarios you have written these last two days. Which possible outcomes can you actually control and which are outside your control?

Circle those possible outcomes that, while they may or may not happen, you cannot assure will or will not come about; that is, the possible outcomes that are beyond your control.

How are you led to pray after doing this exercise?

_____
_____
_____
_____
_____
_____
_____
_____
_____

EVENING: Use your imagination to see and experience the most likely scenario. Using the imagination helps make a possible future more real to the brain. Our neurons don't know the difference between what is real and what is imagined. That's why a person can wake up from a bad dream in a cold sweat; the brain experienced the dream as real. So imagine your most likely scenario coming to pass. See it. Experience it. Pre-live it.

Describe what it was like imagining this future. What did you feel? What did you notice? What did you learn?

_____
_____
_____
_____
_____
_____
_____
_____

Galatians 6:8 reads, "Whoever sows to please their flesh, from the flesh will reap destruction." Do you see this verse being an accurate forecast in your scenarios?

_____
_____
_____
_____
_____
_____
_____

What do you find yourself desiring to pray about?

_____
_____
_____
_____
_____
_____

DAY 3

MORNING: You have considered what might happen if you ignore the alarm. Now consider what might happen should you choose to respond to the alarm with Awakening, Honesty, and Action.

For example, Claire could wake up to her selfishness, honestly assess the hurt she is causing, and take action by returning to Walter and Amber, asking for forgiveness, and starting a process of working through her negative spirit.

However, even if a person does heed the alarm, many possible scenarios might come to pass. If you answer the alarm in your life, what might be the **best possible scenario?**

For Claire, the best scenario might be that Walter and Amber would welcome her back with understanding and compassion. The family would work through their issues and achieve a stronger bond than ever before. Claire could learn the secret of being content in all situations. Her dissatisfaction could drain away. She could find herself truly happy.

If you heed your alarm, what is the best possible scenario?

_____

_____

_____

_____

_____

_____

_____

_____

_____

_____

_____

_____

_____

_____

_____

After writing this scenario out, what do you find yourself wanting to pray about?

_____

_____

_____

_____

_____

_____

EVENING: Responding to an alarm doesn't automatically mean everything in life is going to get better. Sometimes things get worse.

Walter and Amber might reject Claire's approaches. They might rally friends and family against Claire, so that she is isolated. She might try to work on herself but find it difficult to overcome her negative, demanding, dissatisfied spirit. Brad might move on, too, so Claire finds herself divorced and lonely even after deciding to do the right thing.

The apostle Paul woke up to his wrongs and wholly turned himself over to Jesus. Read some of the consequences of his AHA in 2 Corinthians 11:23–28.

What might be the **worst possible scenario** should you respond to your alarm?

_____

_____

_____

_____

_____

_____

_____

_____

_____

_____

What do you find yourself saying to God?

DAY 4

MORNING: Should you heed this alarm, what is the **most likely scenario?**

If Claire returned to Walter and Amber with deep remorse and continued to pursue restoration with them while working on her own self-absorbed personality, it is likely that Walter and Amber would, in time, forgive her and even re-establish the family. It is likely there would be a lot of pain and bumps along the way, but it is also likely that a marriage that labors through such an ordeal would be stronger and more vital.

What is the most likely scenario should you respond whole-heartedly to your alarm? Include:

- how your character will be affected
- how your relationships will be affected
- how others will be affected

_____
_____
_____
_____
_____
_____
_____
_____
_____
_____
_____
_____
_____
_____
_____
_____
_____
_____
_____
_____

Look back over the last three scenarios. Which of the possible consequences do you have control over and which do you not? Circle those over which you don't have power, no matter what you do.

How do you find yourself led to pray?

_____

_____

_____

_____

_____

_____

_____

_____

_____

EVENING: Use your imagination to experience the most likely events should you answer the alarm. See it in your mind's eye. Pre-live the scenario.

Describe what it was like imagining this future. What did you feel? What did you notice? What did you learn?

_____

_____

_____

_____

_____

_____

_____

_____

Galatians 6:8 begins, "Whoever sows to please their flesh, from the flesh will reap destruction" and concludes, "whoever sows to please the Spirit, from the Spirit will reap eternal life." Do you see this saying to hold true in your future scenarios?

_____

_____

_____

_____

_____

_____

_____

What effect does writing and imagining these scenarios have on your inclination toward the alarm?

_____

_____

_____

_____

_____

_____

_____

How do you find yourself being led to pray?

_____

_____

_____

_____

_____

_____

_____

_____

DAY 5

MORNING: Today, think about which scenario you would most likely live out if you came from the perspective of each zone in the honesty/compassion matrix.

Begin with the "dishonesty/condemnation" zone in the bottom right corner. In this zone our dishonesty tends to take the form of exaggerating our faults. We exaggerate our faults because this feels right when under a spirit of condemnation. In this zone we tend to say to ourselves things such as, "What's wrong with me? Everything I do is wrong. I never get anything right. It's hopeless. I don't know how God could ever love me." If you were in this zone, which scenario from the six options on page 59 would you most likely live out? Write it in that zone on the diagram.

Next, imagine being in the "dishonesty/compassion" zone on the bottom left. In this zone we tend to feel sorry for ourselves out of a feeling of compassion, and so we minimize our faults. We tend to say to ourselves things such as, "Sure I've got some problems, but I'm better than most people. Who could blame me for what I'm doing anyway, with all I've been through in my life? God's lucky I'm not a lot worse. And if God wanted me to change, he would give me more help. I'm really doing the best I can." If you were in that zone, which of the six scenarios would you most likely live out? Write it in that zone on the diagram.

Now see yourself in the "honesty/condemnation" zone on the top right. In this state we tend to tell ourselves the truth, but with a spirit of judgment or contempt. We tend to say things such as, "I have done some good things but I have also done some really bad things. There is no excuse for those. I've got to pay for my rebellion and stupidity. I should have changed a long time ago. And until I get fixed, I don't deserve anything good in my life. God is right to be ticked at me." If you were in this zone, which scenario would you most likely live out? Write it in that area on the diagram.

Finally, picture yourself in the "honesty/compassion" zone at the top left. Here we tend to tell ourselves the full truth but with a sense of understanding and grace. We tend to say things to ourselves such as, "This part of my life isn't healthy; it's destroying me. There are good reasons I'm like this, and it is hard to change. But I don't need to stay here. I will ask for forgiveness again and believe my loving Father does forgive. Then I will find a way with his help to work through this issue in order to realize the better life he wants for me. While I am struggling, I will continue to trust God's loving grace." If you were in this zone, toward which scenario would you be drawn?

THE SIX OPTIONS

1. Ignore the alarm and expect the worst possible scenario to occur

2. Ignore the alarm and expect the best possible scenario to occur

3. Ignore the alarm and expect the most likely scenario to occur

4. Respond to the alarm and expect the best possible scenario to occur

5. Respond to the alarm and expect the worst possible scenario to occur

6. Respond to the alarm and expect the most likely scenario to occur

	COMPASSION	CONDEMNATION
HONEST		
DISHONEST		

Which zone do you want to be in today?

_____

_____

_____

_____

_____

Imagine one situation you are likely to be in today, and see yourself responding from the honesty/compassion zone.

Take this picture with you today.

EVENING: Which zone did you find yourself primarily living out of today, and why?

_____

_____

_____

_____

_____

What was the fruit of living out of that zone?

_____

_____

_____

_____

_____

Did you find yourself responding to the alarm you have been considering in any particular way? If so, what was it like?

_____

_____

_____

_____

_____

Take a moment to think about others in your group. For those you know well enough, which zone would you say each one tends to live out of? Jot their initials in that zone.

	COMPASSION	CONDEMNATION
HONEST		
DISHONEST		

Considering that these folks are doing the same exercises you are, how will you pray for each one?

_____

_____

_____

_____

_____

_____

_____

_____

_____

_____

_____

_____

_____

_____

_____

_____

_____

_____

_____

_____

_____

_____

_____

_____

_____

_____

_____

_____

_____

SESSION

4

DVD Presentation

Use the space below to write your reflections or thoughts on this episode.

aha

Tribe 3 in gradients. — 1) sudden awakening; 2) brutal
honesty 3) immediate action

3 - words
1. I have sinned & ..

DAILY EXERCISES

DAY 1

MORNING: Look at yourself in a mirror, a full-length mirror if possible.
Avoid changing anything about yourself as you look. Don't straighten your
hair or adjust your makeup. Slowly scan your physical self. Start at the
lowest part of your body visible in the mirror. Move your gaze gradually
upward until you reach the top of your head. Notice what you see, but also
notice your reaction to what you see. For greater effect try this exercise
without the camouflage of clothing.

Write your feelings and thoughts following this exercise.

Consider the matrix below.

☐ **Zone 1:** Were you honest about your appearance, grateful for what is good, and compassionate toward what is less than perfect?

☐ **Zone 2:** Were you honest about your appearance, but with a sense of disgust or judgment toward what is less than perfect?

☐ **Zone 3:** Were you less than honest about yourself by focusing on only your positive traits and avoiding looking at the less than perfect?

☐ **Zone 4:** Were you less than honest with yourself by focusing mostly on your negative traits and skipping over your positive features?

Draw a stick figure in the zone where you found yourself while considering yourself in the mirror.

	COMPASSION	CONDEMNATION
HONEST	**1**	**2**
DISHONEST	**3**	**4**

What prayer arises out of your heart after this exercise?

_____
_____
_____
_____

Whenever you look at yourself in the mirror today, recall this exercise.

_____
_____
_____
_____
_____

EVENING: Stand before the mirror again, and read aloud Psalm 103:13–14 (New American Standard Bible):

Just as a father has compassion on his children,
    So the LORD has compassion on those who fear Him.
For He Himself knows our frame;
    He is mindful that we are but dust.

Carry out the same exercise described this morning. But this time perform it while intentionally cultivating a spirit of honest compassion toward yourself.

Write what observing yourself with honest compassion was like.

_____
_____
_____
_____
_____
_____
_____
_____
_____
_____
_____
_____

How will you pray?

_____
_____
_____
_____
_____
_____
_____
_____

DAY 2

MORNING: Each day the rest of this week, you will be encouraged to experiment with looking at yourself in the mirror and telling yourself the truth about your AHA from the perspective of one of the four zones.

Today you will start with Zone 4 at the bottom right, dishonest condemnation. Or course, in this zone we don't actually tell ourselves the truth, but we often think we do. When in this mindset we are against ourselves. We stand in judgement on ourselves. We beat ourselves up. And being under condemnation, we exaggerate our faults and ignore our good points.

So, when it comes to the alarm you have been considering, what would you say to yourself if you were in the bottom right area? Write it below:

_____
_____
_____
_____
_____
_____
_____
_____
_____
_____

Standing in front of a mirror, look in your eyes and tell yourself what you just wrote. Say aloud to yourself the things you would normally say silently to yourself if you were in Zone 4.

Write your reaction.

_____
_____
_____
_____
_____
_____
_____

Try to stay in Zone 4 today. Notice what it is like. Wake up to the effect being in Zone 4 has on your disposition, your energy, and your motivation.

EVENING: What was it like being in Zone 4 today?

_____

_____

_____

_____

_____

_____

_____

_____

_____

How do you tend to pray when in Zone 4?

_____

_____

_____

_____

_____

Do you think God wants you in Zone 4? Why or why not?

_____

_____

_____

_____

_____

Close your day by reflecting on Luke 5:1–11.

_____

_____

_____

_____

_____

DAY 3

MORNING: Today, put yourself in Zone 3, the bottom left zone, dishonest compassion.

Create a sense of compassion for yourself, and out of that compassion, exaggerate your virtues and minimize your wrongs when it comes to your AHA. Write below what you would say to yourself about your AHA from the perspective of dishonest compassion.

_____
_____
_____
_____
_____
_____
_____
_____
_____
_____

Stand in front of the mirror and tell yourself what you just wrote, "the truth" from this vantage point. Look yourself in the eyes and speak aloud.

Write your reaction to this experience.

_____
_____
_____
_____
_____
_____
_____
_____
_____

Try to stay in Zone 3 today. Notice what it is like. See the effect being in dishonest compassion has on your disposition, your energy, and your motivation.

EVENING: What was it like being in Zone 3 today?

_____
_____
_____
_____
_____
_____
_____

How do you pray when in Zone 3?

_____
_____
_____
_____
_____
_____

Do you think God wants you in Zone 3? Why or why not?

_____
_____
_____
_____
_____

Close your day by reflecting on 1 John 1:8–10:

If we claim to be without sin,
we deceive ourselves and the truth is not in us.

If we confess our sins, he is faithful and just
and will forgive us our sins and purify us from all unrighteousness.

If we claim we have not sinned,
we make him out to be a liar and his word is not in us.

DAY 4

MORNING: Today, put yourself in Zone 2, the top right space, honest condemnation.

Be as honest as you can about the truth of your AHA. Also generate a sense of condemnation toward your failure and toward yourself for failing. Write below what you would say to yourself when in this zone.

_____
_____
_____
_____
_____
_____
_____
_____
_____

Stand before a mirror and tell yourself what you just wrote, "the truth" from this vantage point. Look yourself in the eyes and speak aloud.

Write your reaction to this exercise.

_____
_____
_____
_____
_____
_____
_____
_____
_____

Try to stay in Zone 2 today. Notice what it is like. Observe the effect living in candid condemnation has on your disposition, your energy, and your motivation.

EVENING: What was it like being in Zone 2 today?

_____

_____

_____

_____

_____

_____

_____

_____

_____

How do you find yourself praying when in Zone 2?

_____

_____

_____

_____

_____

Do you think God wants you in Zone 2? Why or why not?

_____

_____

_____

_____

_____

Close by reflecting on these two Scripture passages:

If our hearts condemn us,
we know that God is greater than our hearts,
and he knows everything (1 John 3:20).

I care very little if I am judged by you or by any human court;
 indeed, I do not even judge myself (1 Corinthians 4:3).

DAY 5

MORNING: Today, put yourself in the top left zone, Zone 1, honest compassion.

Be as honest as you can about the reality of your alarm. Also generate a sense of gentleness, compassion, and understanding toward yourself. Write below what you say to yourself from the outlook of Zone 1.

_____

_____

_____

_____

_____

_____

_____

_____

_____

_____

Stand in front of the mirror and tell yourself what you just wrote the truth with this spirit. Look yourself in the eyes and speak aloud.

Write your reaction.

_____

_____

_____

_____

_____

Try to stay in Zone 1 today. Notice what it is like to live in total honesty and total compassion. Wake up to the effect being in Zone 1 has on your disposition, your energy, and your motivation.

EVENING: What was it like being in Zone 1 today?

_____

_____

_____

How do you find yourself praying when in Zone 1?

_____
_____
_____
_____
_____
_____

Do you think God wants you in Zone 1? Why or why not?

_____
_____
_____
_____
_____

Close by reflecting on these verses from Romans 7:24—8:1 and 8:31–34:

What a wretched man I am!
Who will rescue me from this body that is subject to death?
Thanks be to God, who delivers me through Jesus Christ our Lord!

So then, I myself in my mind am a slave to God's law,
but in my sinful nature a slave to the law of sin.
Therefore, there is now no condemnation for those who are in Christ Jesus.

What, then, shall we say in response to these things?
If God is for us, who can be against us?
He who did not spare his own Son, but gave him up for us all—
how will he not also, along with him, graciously give us all things?

Who will bring any charge against those whom God has chosen?
It is God who justifies.
Who then is the one who condemns?
No one.
Christ Jesus who died—more than that, who was raised to life—
is at the right hand of God and is also interceding for us.

SESSION

5

DVD Presentation

Use the space below to write your reflections or thoughts on this episode.

_____

_____

_____

_____

_____

_____

_____

_____

_____

_____

_____

_____

_____

_____

_____

_____

_____

_____

_____

_____

	COMPASSION	CONDEMNATION
HONEST	1	2
DISHONEST	3	4

DAILY EXERCISES

DAY 1

MORNING: The purpose of this week's exercises is to decide on an Action related to your AHA.

Is there an obvious Action in relation to your Awareness and Honesty? If so, what is it?

_____
_____
_____
_____
_____
_____

If you see an obvious action, will you take the action today, even right now? Why or why not?

_____
_____
_____
_____
_____
_____

If you do not see an obvious action, read Acts 9:1–6. Note what stands out to you.

_____
_____
_____
_____
_____

In his AHA experience, Paul did take the immediate action of going on to Damascus. But then he had to wait for what came next. If you are truly not sure what action is appropriate in your AHA, maybe your first action is to "go to Damascus"; that is, wait, be open, and listen. Are you willing to do that this week? What are your thoughts?

Express those thoughts to Jesus.

_____

_____

_____

_____

_____

_____

_____

_____

Are you willing to take the action of asking Jesus for direction in what step to take next?

☐ Yes, because... ☐ Not really, because...

_____

_____

_____

_____

_____

_____

Today, be alert to guidance on what might be your next action.

EVENING: During this day, did you find yourself being directed in what action to take in regard to your AHA? If so, what did you "hear"?

_____

_____

_____

_____

_____

_____

_____

_____

_____

_____

Are you willing to act on what seems to be a direction for you? Why or why not?

_____
_____
_____
_____
_____

If you didn't notice any direction, then brainstorm a list of the possible actions that come to mind.

_____
_____
_____
_____
_____
_____
_____

As you made the list, did any actions stand out? If so, which one(s)?

_____
_____
_____
_____

Look over your list, imagining Jesus right beside you. What effect or direction does picturing him alongside you provide?

_____
_____
_____
_____

How do you find yourself being led to pray?

_____
_____
_____
_____

DAY 2

MORNING: If an action has yet to truly stand out, then make a list of pros and cons related to each possible action by filling in the chart below.

Possible Action

_____

_____

Pros

_____

_____

Cons

_____

_____

Possible Action

_____

_____

Pros

_____

_____

Cons

_____

_____

Possible Action

_____

_____

Pros

_____

_____

Cons

_____

_____

EVENING: Look back over your pros and cons. What stands out to you? What do you notice?

_____

_____

_____

_____

_____

_____

_____

_____

_____

Did this exercise help you decide what action is best?

_____

_____

_____

_____

_____

_____

How do you find yourself being led to pray?

_____

_____

_____

_____

_____

DAY 3

MORNING: Today you will look over your possible actions in light of the honesty matrix. So far this week, as you have considered your possible actions, which zone have you found yourself in for the most part?

☐ Zone 1: Honesty with compassion
☐ Zone 2: Honesty with condemnation
☐ Zone 3: Dishonesty with compassion
☐ Zone 4: Dishonesty with condemnation

What signs or evidence lead you to believe that you have been primarily in this zone?

_____

_____

_____

_____

_____

_____

_____

What effect has being in that zone had on your thinking and your feelings in regard to this action?

_____

_____

_____

_____

_____

If, for the most part, you have not been in Zone 1, how would being in that top left zone shape or change your thoughts and feelings about what action to take?

_____

_____

_____

_____

_____

_____

_____

Read John 1:17 aloud.

> For the law was given through Moses;
> grace and truth came through Jesus Christ.

Read it aloud a couple more times.

If a person was living under the Law of Moses, which zone(s) would he likely find himself in? Explain your thinking.

_____

_____

_____

_____

_____

_____

_____

_____

If a person was living under the grace and truth of Jesus, which zone(s) would he likely find himself in? Explain your reasoning.

_____

_____

_____

_____

_____

_____

_____

_____

When you consider which zone you typically find yourself in, which would you say you have been living under, for all practical purposes: the Law of Moses or the grace and truth of Jesus? Describe what leads you to think so.

_____

_____

_____

_____

_____

_____

_____

_____

_____

Write John 1:17 on a card or slip of paper. Look at it often during your day. Each time you look at it, read the sentence aloud. Each time you do, emphasize a different word in the sentence.

EVENING: What came from reading John 1:17 aloud multiple times?

_____
_____
_____
_____
_____
_____
_____
_____

Turn to John 8. As you read verses 2–11, notice the use of the words law and condemn.

Into which zone did the Law of Moses put this woman?

_____
_____
_____
_____

Into which zone did the Law of Moses put her accusers?

_____
_____
_____
_____
_____

Into which zone did Jesus put this woman?

_____
_____
_____
_____
_____

Jesus commanded the woman to take action. Out of which zone on the matrix was he urging her to take action? State your reasoning.

_____

_____

_____

_____

_____

_____

_____

What if Jesus had said, "They don't condemn you, but I condemn you. Now go and stop sinning so you avoid any further condemnation. And maybe in time, if you can become righteous, you can break out of condemnation"? How might that have changed the effect of the story?

_____

_____

_____

_____

_____

_____

_____

If Jesus had said those alternate words, how might it have affected what actions the woman would have taken next?

_____

_____

_____

_____

_____

If you heard the true words of John 8:11 for yourself in regard to your AHA, what would you do next?

_____

_____

_____

_____

_____

DAY 4

MORNING: Today you are encouraged to choose a definite action in relation to your AHA, even if you are not sure it is the best action.

Choose an action. Write it here.

Before taking the action, test it with the following four questions:

1. **Is this action actually a delay tactic, an action to avoid action?**

A person might decide to take action, for example, by ordering a book that speaks to her AHA issue. Reading a book could be a true step forward. But it might also be a simple attempt to put off doing what she knows she should do, such as making an appointment with a counselor or writing a letter of apology. So is this action a true action for you or is it a pseudo-action to avoid the true action? Explain your thinking.

_____

_____

_____

_____

_____

_____

_____

_____

2. **Am I taking this action just to make myself feel better?**

People make themselves feel better by punishing themselves. They stop eating or refuse to hang out with friends or give away money to, in effect, pay for what they have done. People also make themselves feel better by doing something to prove they are worthy again. They might recommit at church, go on a mission trip, or start an intensive Bible study. Is the action you choose something to pacify your guilt or a true turning toward the Father?

_____

_____

_____

_____

_____

_____

_____

_____

3. **Is this action loving toward others?**

It may not be loving to tell your spouse about an emotional affair at work or tell a friend all the bad things you've been saying about her behind her back. Does the action you choose include compassion toward others?

_____

_____

_____

_____

_____

_____

_____

4. **Is this action birthed out of a trust in the compassion of Jesus?**

_____

_____

_____

_____

_____

_____

_____

If these questions submarined the action you thought to take, choose a different action and run it through the same four tests. writing your responses below.

_____

_____

_____

_____

_____

_____

_____

_____

_____

_____

Based on the tests, choose an action. Write it here.

_____

_____

_____

_____

_____

Sit with this action today. See how it resonates with you, whether you sense confirmation or caution.

EVENING: How did sitting with this action today affect you? What did you notice?

_____

_____

_____

_____

_____

_____

_____

_____

If you are still unsure what action to take, would you be willing to discuss it with a trusted friend? Proverbs 15:22 says, "Plans fail for lack of counsel, but with many advisers they succeed." But not all advisors are equal. All the characters in the video got bad advice from friends.

Think through your closest friends. As you do, ask yourself if they are honest or dishonest with you. Also ask if they tend toward compassion or condemnation. Place each one's name on the matrix based on your experience.

	COMPASSION	CONDEMNATION
HONEST	1	2
DISHONEST	3	4

Does a name stand out as one in which you could confide and seek direction? If so, write it below, and when you will make contact.

_____

_____

_____

_____

_____

How do you find yourself being led to pray?

_____

_____

_____

_____

_____

DAY 5

MORNING: "When are you going to get up?" Choose today to get up and actually take action related to your AHA.

Write out how you will take the action you have now chosen: when, where, and exactly what you will do. If you still aren't sure about an action, then commit to talking to a trusted friend.

_____

_____

_____

_____

_____

_____

_____

_____

_____

_____

_____

_____

Ask for the power to follow through.

Believe you have the power to follow through (even if you aren't sure you have it).

EVENING: Complete the sentences below to describe what it was like taking action today.

Before taking the action, I thought and felt...

_____

_____

_____

While taking the action, I thought and felt...

_____

_____

_____

After taking the action, I thought and felt…

_____

_____

_____

What do you see or learn from answering these questions?

_____

_____

_____

_____

_____

_____

_____

We can never be 100 percent sure a particular action was the best choice. Can you give yourself compassion even if this action doesn't turn out as you hope?

_____

_____

_____

_____

_____

_____

_____

How are you lead to pray?

_____

_____

_____

_____

_____

_____

_____

_____

NOTES:

SESSION

6

COMING HOME

DVD Presentation

Use the space below to write your reflections or thoughts on this episode.

_____

_____

_____

_____

_____

_____

_____

_____

_____

_____

_____

_____

_____

_____

_____

_____

_____

_____

Carmen: May I take you order please?

Anjela: Carmen, can we just talk? I know you're angry.

Carmen: Yeah, you're very sensitive to other people's feelings.

Anjela: I'm just trying to say I'm sorry.

Carmen: Like they told you to do in rehab? Which of the twelve steps is making amends? You'll have to tell me because I've never been to rehab, because I've never been addicted, because I was too busy staying home, doing my job, looking after Dad. But hey! You said sorry, so I guess I have to stop being mad now.

STAYING HOME

The action needed to come home from the far country may be simple, but oftentimes staying home doesn't seem so simple. Furthermore, not becoming lost while at home can be downright tricky.

That is why your journal includes this follow-up section called "Staying Home."

The purpose of this extra section is to help you discover a way of life that produces ongoing Awakenings, increasing Honesty, and constructive Actions—AHAs that will connect you ever more deeply to the relentless, reckless love of the Father. Then you will be less likely to leave home.

"STAYING HOME" IS BUILT ON THESE TEN SUPPOSITIONS:

1. While life with the Father is a gift, the vitality of this life is either enhanced or diminished through daily habits.

Just as physical life is a gift—you didn't do anything to receive it, you were just born—your spiritual life is also a gift. You were born again by the grace of God.

Your physical life can be diminished (or even ended) by your habits. If you eat too much and exercise too little, smoke too much and sleep too little, or work too much and play too little, you may not physically die, but the life energy inside you will certainly dwindle.

You can also enhance the physical life you have been given through wise habits. Your control over the vitality of your physical life is not absolute, however. Other factors affect your vigor: heredity, environment, disease, and so on. But the influence your habits have on the quality of your physical life is substantial.

The same principle holds true with your spiritual life. Your relationship with the Father is a gift. But the vitality of this relationship will be determined, in part, by how you nourish it or neglect it. Choosing wise practices that enhance your grace-based relationship with the Father will help you stay home and love home.

2. Everyone is different. So the practices that build life with the Father will be different for everyone.

Good parents understand that each of their children connects in unique ways. One daughter connects with her father by sitting on his lap and reading a story. Another daughter feels restless and confined sitting still, even with a loving father. She connects better by riding bikes or going fishing.

Similarly, what connects one child of God to the Father's love is often different from what connects another. One child can sit with the Father for an hour reading the Scripture story and feel united. Another daughter of God may find that same practice uninspiring and even draining. But let this second child walk in nature, pondering a verse such as, "The heavens declare the glory of God; the skies proclaim the work of his hands" (Psalms 19:1), and her heart fills with the love of the Father.

Embracing this principle frees you to find the ways you best meet and know the Father, which leads to Principle 3.

3. Experimenting with what practices best connect you to the Father will enhance your spiritual life and the likelihood you will stay home.

If you felt unqualified permission to experiment with what activities connect you most deeply to the Father's love, what would you try? What might you do? In essence, you become your own research lab. You put different practices in the test tube of your experience and see what results.

What happens when you turn the worship music on your car stereo up to ten and sing along? What is it like to spend fifteen minutes at sunset on your back deck in prayer and reflection? What occurs in your heart when you volunteer at the homeless shelter? What comes of taking part in your small group?

Isn't this how good relationships really work, after all? When a couple is dating, they try different activities together. They might discover they connect to each other when they work out together or take a long drive. They might discover that attending a sporting event or shopping at the mall actually disconnects them even though they do it together. Wise couples adjust their activities in light of what nourishes their connection.

This principle leads to the following corollary.

4. Beware of blindly following what others tell you is the way you ought to connect to the Father.

Here is a typical scenario that destroys life with the Father rather than enhancing it.

Jim has a powerful AHA. When he comes back to the Father, someone tells him that he should begin each day waking thirty minutes early for devotions. He should read the Bible for fifteen minutes and then pray for fifteen minutes. He starts that habit and finds it clarifying, inspiring, and invaluable. He assumes this is how everyone should meet with the Father.

So when Jim's friend, Shane, has an AHA and tells Jim about it, Jim tells him that he simply must get up thirty minutes early every day for Bible reading and prayer. This is the way to meet with the Father. It's worked for him, after all.

Shane sees the power this practice has in Jim's life. So he commits to getting up thirty minutes early for reading and prayer. But to Shane, this practice feels like drudgery. It feels empty. When he is honest, it feels like death. He begins to dread mornings.

Shane wonders, "What is wrong with me? I ought to love the Bible." Feeling guilty about his failure, Shane begins to avoid not just his devotions, but the Father as well. He secretly starts to resent the Father for demanding what feels like a monotonous routine (even though it wasn't the Father who demanded it). Shane's false guilt and growing bitterness become his first steps of wandering away from home all over again.

Or possibly worse, if Shane sticks with the morning practice despite its dreariness, his very determination can be the beginning of becoming the older brother. Shane might find himself saying, "I read my Bible whether I like it or not. If I can do it, anyone can. People who don't stick it out just aren't trying."

Notice Shane's focus is now on reading the Bible, not meeting with the Father; on doing the "right thing" rather than on living in the Father's love. In a seeming contradiction, the habit of morning Bible reading is causing Shane to be more lost than found.

But that should not be a surprise. Life is not in Bible reading, nor in any particular practice you perform. According to 1 John 5:11, "Life is in his Son."

This leads us to our fifth principle.

5. If your spiritual practices are not leading you toward the Father's heart, toward greater love, joy, and peace, they aren't spiritual practices, they are merely religious rituals.

Any religious practice that is not building life with the Father through the Son is dangerous. Any habit that isn't drawing you into the zone of honest compassion is a trap. It doesn't matter how "good" and "foundational" the practice is supposed to be. Every practice is just that, a practice. It is not god. It is not life.

6. Some practices may be "targeted," that is, pointed at a particular weakness or area of growth.

When you report a sickness to your doctor, you expect medication targeted toward that illness. When you employ a personal trainer to prepare to run a marathon, you expect targeted training exercises leading to that goal. It is the same with spiritual healing and growth.

Say that during Corey's AHA, he discovers he is quite arrogant and self-centered. What could he do? Going to church and reading the Bible may help in a general way, but what would target his pride? Corey could experiment with practices that might "treat" this flawed aspect of his character. Secret acts of service or regular confession of sin may be the best medicines.

If during Paige's AHA, she realizes she is deeply shame-filled, what might she do? She may need, in a sense, to do the opposite of what Corey does. She may need to intentionally allow others to compliment her and serve her, even though it is uncomfortable. Learning to receive unconditional love is what she needs. To be proactive, she might need to stop meeting with the toxic friend who abuses her heart and schedule time with a friend who unconditionally loves her.

Targeting spiritual practices can intensify the effect of your practices.

7. Evaluate your spiritual practices by their fruit.

Jesus said a good tree produces good fruit. Paul said that the fruit of the Spirit is love, joy, and peace. So evaluate your habits by this criterion: what fruit is the practice producing?

If a practice cultivates love, joy, and peace within, if it draws you into Zone 1, then it is a spiritual practice. It doesn't matter whether or not others consider the practice to be spiritual. If a practice fills you with the Spirit of the Father, it is spiritual.

If, on the other hand, you find that a practice is building pride, superiority, self-reliance, or shame in you—that is, if it is leaving you in a zone other than Zone 1—then the practice isn't spiritual. The practice is best modified or purged.

8. Since the purpose is to live in the Father's love and not just follow some prescribed list of rules, you can feel free to be creative in how you connect with him.

Galatians 5:1 says, "It is for freedom that Christ has set us free. Stand firm, then, and do not let yourselves be burdened again by a yoke of slavery."

You can be enslaved to sin, as you may have discovered in the far country. But you can also be enslaved to oughts, shoulds, and musts, rules that have little connection to your relationship to the Father. It is through legalism that you can become the older brother. It is from the wooden adherence to the law that Paul is saying you are free.

Paul further says we are liberated to "live by the Spirit." That means you are at liberty to discover how you connect to the Father. You are free to learn what gives you life. The practices will likely involve traditional ingredients such as prayer, worship, service, and so on. But how you engage in these fundamental ingredients will be as varied as the noses on our faces.

So you can be open to what the Spirit will show you as to how best to connect with the Father through the Son. Is it through energetic worship? Is it through quiet meditation? Is it through serving the poor? Is it through challenging the rich? Is it through large-group classes? Is it though solo encounters with a mentor? Is it some of the above or even all the above?

Whatever connects you to the Father's love, joy, and peace; those are your holy habits.

9. Experimenting and testing your practices is an ongoing lifestyle. Different practices have different values at different points in your journey.

The little girl who, at age five, found great connection to her father by reading on his lap may find that pastime to be less meaningful as she grows. She may find that taking a walk with her daddy while talking about her day now connects her in a deeper fashion.

In the same way, a child of God may realize that a recovery group that was life-giving after her divorce loses its effect as she heals. Replacing the support group with a service group may connect her best with the Father during the next chapter of her story.

It is also true that some practices simply lose their effect over time just because you get used to them. They become routine. In a sense, you build a tolerance to the practice. The first time a person runs a mile, it may create a dramatic physical effect. But to run a mile every day and never change the regimen will lead to a decrease in the value. To switch up the distance and to slot in other forms of exertion will stimulate greater effects. In the same way, altering spiritual practices can improve their value.

Some habits, however, may be beneficial for a lifetime. The little girl who connected with her father while fishing may always connect with him in this way. The child of God who connects with the Father through morning devotions may always meaningfully connect with him in that fashion.

To stay awake to the effect that spiritual practices are having upon you is essential to maintaining a vital connection to the Father's heart.

10. You don't do spiritual practices because you are spiritual. You do spiritual practices because you are not.

Your spiritual practices are not proof that you are more spiritual than others. Just the opposite. They are a humble admission that without the influx of life that comes from these practices, you will inevitably lose your fire and stray from home. The truth is, most of us are not Awake to just how many sources of connection with the Father we need to sustain a fullness of spirit.

The "saints" who are known to pray for hours, regularly fast, or live in simplicity are not inherently more spiritual than the rest of us. They are just more humble, that is, more Awake to their need for help.

This is why the Scriptures encourage you with admonitions such as, "Pray without ceasing." The command is not setting some lofty bar of righteousness. It is an encouragement to recognize that your need for the Father's love and power is so daily, so hourly, so moment-by-moment.

Someone might object to these "Staying Home" principles, saying, "We shouldn't spend so much time focusing on ourselves! Isn't the Christian life about others?" Notice that while this objection sounds humble and holy, pride is smuggled into the center of it. Out of which zone would a person make such an objection? The assumption hidden inside the objection is that we are strong enough to be always giving, always loving, always others-centered on our own, as if we were superhuman. The assumption is that we have little need for help, which is a very dangerous assumption.

WHAT "STAYING HOME" INVOLVES

The Staying Home strategy includes three components:

1. AN INITIAL SELF-APPRAISAL

This self-evaluation guides you in considering the effect of your current spiritual practices and choosing those to keep and those to modify or stop. The evaluation also helps you consider what other practices might connect you to the Father.

2. AN EIGHT-WEEK LOG

You are challenged to keep a daily log of your spiritual practices, noting their real effects. This daily review should take only about five minutes. On the following pages, week 1 has been provided for you. Follow this format for the remaining 7 weeks on separate sheets of paper or email info@cityonahillstudio.com to receive a free 7-week pdf of the logs.

At the end of each week, you will be prompted to evaluate the practices of the week and make appropriate adjustments.

3. GROUP REPORT AND SUPPORT

During this eight weeks, whenever your group meets, each person is allowed two minutes to report his or her findings from the log. Describing aloud what you are discovering reinforces your efforts and clarifies your thoughts.

THE INITIAL APPRAISAL

1. In the left-hand column list your spiritual practices or holy habits: church participation, Bible reading, forms of prayer, service commitments, study groups, and so forth. Include both regular practices and the more occasional ones, such as an annual mission trip or fall retreat.

PRACTICES	FRUIT	ZONE

2. Include in the list above any other activities or habits that connect you to the Father or fill you with life even if they aren't considered traditional spiritual practices. If, for example, when you garden you find yourself delighting in the love of God, then add gardening to the list. Or say you notice that riding your motorcycle makes you feel grateful and connected; then add it to the list.

3. Note the "fruit" of each of activity. What tends to result when you engage this practice? Are you filled with the Spirit, with love, life, and joy? Do you love the Father more because of this practice? Or does it lead toward self-righteousness, judgment, or pride? Or does the practice leave you empty and listless?

4. At the far right, note which of the four zones on the matrix this activity tends to reinforce.

5. Begin a list of practices or activities that you think might fill you with greater life, love for God, and compassion for others by completing the sentences below.

- Things I have always wanted to try:

_____

_____

_____

_____

_____

_____

- Things I used to do that gave me life, but I stopped:

_____

_____

_____

_____

_____

_____

- Things outside the "strictly spiritual" but may fill me with the power of his love (We are, after all, creatures of body, mind, and soul. We are told to love God with all our heart, mind, soul, and strength. So we will connect to the Father in each of these modes. Practices like long-distance running, playing with children, writing poetry, or reading great literature may connect a person to the Father's love just as much as more customary spiritual disciplines.):

_____

_____

_____

_____

_____

_____

• Traditional spiritual practices that I have never tried, such as weekly fasting, anonymous giving, daily solitude, intentional confession, and others:

_____

_____

_____

_____

_____

_____

_____

• Listen to the Spirit. Does any practice or practices arise in your mind that you would not have thought of yourself?

_____

_____

_____

_____

_____

_____

_____

If you feel overwhelmed by "all these things I ought to be doing," remember the idea is not to do all these things because good Christians should do them. The idea is to brainstorm ways you might best connect to the Father's extravagant love and, from the list, experiment with what gives you life.

6. Circle practices you think wise to continue or begin. Put an X beside those you deem wise to curtail.

7. Choose practices you want to try in Week 1. Write them below.

_____

_____

_____

_____

_____

8. Fill in the chart day by day.

Put your journal somewhere you will see it each day. Take five minutes to note your practices from the last twenty-four hours that were intended to connect you to the Father's heart. Note the fruit from each.

You may want to expand this assessment by jotting down all your major activities, just to become more aware of the effect they have on your spirit.

As you make adjustments to your activities, expect criticism from others. If you leave a support group because you realize it is no longer bringing life, others may disapprove or even shame you. If you begin a practice that is outside the norm, others may tease you or frown on it.

Expect internal criticism from yourself as well. An internal voice will likely say things such as, "You're selfish to make time for this. Just suck it up and focus on others. Who else does these silly practices anyway? It's so dumb!" From which zone on the matrix would such a voice arise? Does it sound like the Father's voice?

Finally, while trying these practices, deliberately stay in Zone 1. Be honest about what you experience. Be compassionate toward what you find. If you miss a day (or some days), be gently truthful about it. Learn what you can from the absence. And continue on.

SAMPLE LOG / What I am trying this week:

1. Get to bed no later than 11 P.M. with the idea of getting the sleep I know I need.
2. Play uplifting music during my commute rather than listening to talk radio; maybe even sing along.
3. Take ten minutes at lunch to just sit and be with the Father; listen, pray.
4. Memorize Romans 8:1 about no condemnation. Say it aloud morning and night.
5. Pray with my kids before bed.
6. Walk in the park twice.
7. Make it to small group.
8. Eat lunch one day with my Zone 1 friend.
9. Actually be "awake" during church service; pay attention; look for the Father.
10. Take a real day of rest on Sunday: no work!

Action: What I Did	Honesty: Fruit of the Action	Awareness: Zone
DAY 1: SATURDAY		
Played favorite music on commute	Made me smile!	Zone 1
Called friend about lunch	left message; disappointed that no answer	Zone 2
Tried memorizing verse	frustrated, I can't get it right	Zone 2
Mad at kids; didn't pray with them	mad at self; "I'm a lousy parent"	Zone 4
DAY 2: SUNDAY		
Got to sleep at 11:15 last night	a little more rested than usual; nice!	Zone 1
Church/mostly stayed aware	felt more connected to God; some joy, didn't critique service like I usually do; hung around longer than usual	Zone 1
Friend asked if I wanted to help with youth group... a prompt from the Father?	I might try this, but with an Awareness about whether I find and give life doing it	Zone 2
Did some paperwork today	committed not to work but did anyway, aware of matrix so less in Zone 2 over it	Zone 1/2
Also walked	great to be in nature, felt awesome; I love God!	Zone 1
Friend called back	lunch tomorrow; felt grateful	Zone 1
Prayed with kids; awkward!	still felt better than not doing it	Zone 2/1
DAY 3: MONDAY		
Up past midnight last night	sorry for myself; cranky with everyone else	Zone 3
Tried memorizing again	I'm hopeless	Zone 4
Music during commute	didn't seem to overcome lack of sleep	Zone 2
Lunch with Zone 1 friend	felt seen, known, loved	Zone 1
Drove home the back way; prayed	need to do this more often, settled me, peace	Zone 1
Small group; went, though tired	felt a little more lovable and loving after	Zone 3/1

END OF WEEK OBSERVATIONS (AWARENESS AND HONESTY)

I was hopeful more would happen, but paying attention did help. I wouldn't have had lunch with the friend or taken the one walk (not two) if I hadn't. I simply must spend more time in nature and with this friend. I feel alive with both, sense the fruit of the Spirit, and love God more.

I also notice I am mostly with negative people at work, and even at home. It's essential I make sure to spend time with Zone 1 folks.

Memorizing feels like a burden. It just puts me in "law mode." I'm going to try something else.

Praying with the kids was a mix, so I'm up in the air about it. Am I putting too much pressure on myself to do it because I've heard others do it? I want to keep trying it but be aware of the real effect.

Which zone did you find yourself in most often, and what are the possible factors?
I was probably mostly in Zone 2. I realize lack of sleep, judging myself for not having it all together, and too much work with not enough play all make it hard to get out of that zone.

In which direction on the matrix are you moving?
I would say overall the practices moved me a little toward Zone 1. I had some fresh glimpses of loving and enjoying God and caring more for others. That is where I want to be more and more.

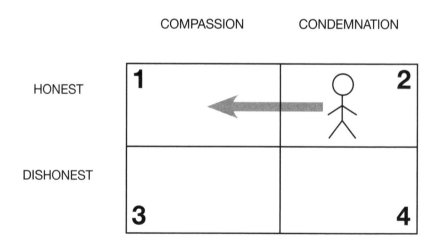

How will you adjust for next week? (Actions)

I will keep having lunch with my Zone 1 friend—every week if I can manage it.
I think three walks a week would be optimal, but how could I ever work it in? Maybe I could walk in the park near work during lunch?

Replace memorizing with choosing one verse a week to keep with me and read aloud during the day, emphasizing different words each time, as we did in the study. I like that better than trying to read a big chunk of the Bible each day.

The rest of the practices I'll keep the same. Oh yeah, and drive home the back way as often as possible.

NOTES:

_____
_____
_____
_____
_____
_____
_____
_____
_____
_____
_____
_____
_____
_____
_____
_____
_____
_____
_____
_____
_____

"I am the vine; you are the branches. If you remain in me and I in you, you will bear much fruit; apart from me you can do nothing."

— **John 15:5**

Action: What I Did	Honesty: Fruit of the Action	Awareness: Zone
DAY 1:		

Action: What I Did	Honesty: Fruit of the Action	Awareness: Zone
DAY 2:		

Action: What I Did	Honesty: Fruit of the Action	Awareness: Zone
DAY 3:		

Action: What I Did	Honesty: Fruit of the Action	Awareness: Zone
DAY 4:		

Action: What I Did	Honesty: Fruit of the Action	Awareness: Zone
DAY 5:		

Action: What I Did	Honesty: Fruit of the Action	Awareness: Zone
DAY 6:		

Action: What I Did	Honesty: Fruit of the Action	Awareness: Zone
DAY 7:		

END OF WEEK OBSERVATIONS (AWARENESS AND HONESTY)

Which zone did you find yourself in most often, and what are the possible factors?

_____

_____

_____

Put a stick figure in that zone.

In which direction on the matrix are you moving?

_____

_____

_____

_____

_____

Draw an arrow indicating that direction.

	COMPASSION	CONDEMNATION
HONEST	1	2
DISHONEST	3	4

How will you adjust for next week? (Actions)

_____

_____

_____

_____

_____

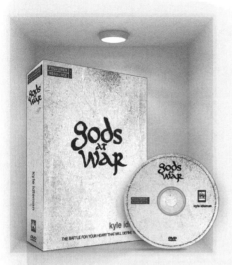

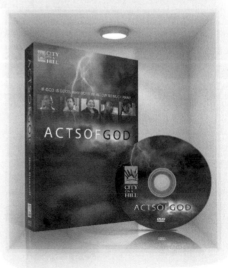